Contents

Wise Publications

Exclusive distributors:
Music Sales Limited
8/9 Frith Street, London W1D 3JB, England.
Music Sales Pty Limited
120 Rothschild Avenue, Rosebery, NSW 2018, Australia.

Order No. AM972653
ISBN 0-7119-9185-5

Written and arranged by Cliff Douse
Edited by Sorcha Armstrong

Book design by Chloë Alexander
Artist photographs courtesy of LFI
Photographs by George Taylor

Printed in the United Kingdom by Caligraving Limited, Thetford, Norfolk.

Foreword

Welcome to the Chord Songbook Starter Book for Guitar.
This book will have you strumming and singing popular songs in next to no time!

Maybe you've got a copy of one of the Guitar Chord Songbooks, and would like to learn authentic-sounding strumming patterns, or perhaps you're a complete beginner just starting out on guitar.

This book has something for everyone, and soon you'll be learning and playing well-known songs and improving your guitar skills! First you'll learn how to tune your guitar, play chords and strum in time with your singing. It will also give you a firm grounding of the popular keys and the chords that sound good in them.

Once you've mastered these few basics, you'll find that there is a wide range of Chord Songbooks available for you to enjoy playing from.

Happy music making!

The guitar

There are two main types of guitar: **acoustic** and **electric**.
Acoustic guitars have a hollow body that naturally amplifies sounds produced by the vibrating strings, while electric instruments, which tend to have solid bodies, use pick-ups to transmit the string sounds to an amplifier.

There are also semi-acoustic guitars, which have both hollow bodies and pick-ups. Acoustic guitars are ideal for folk music, while electrics are essential for most rock and pop music.

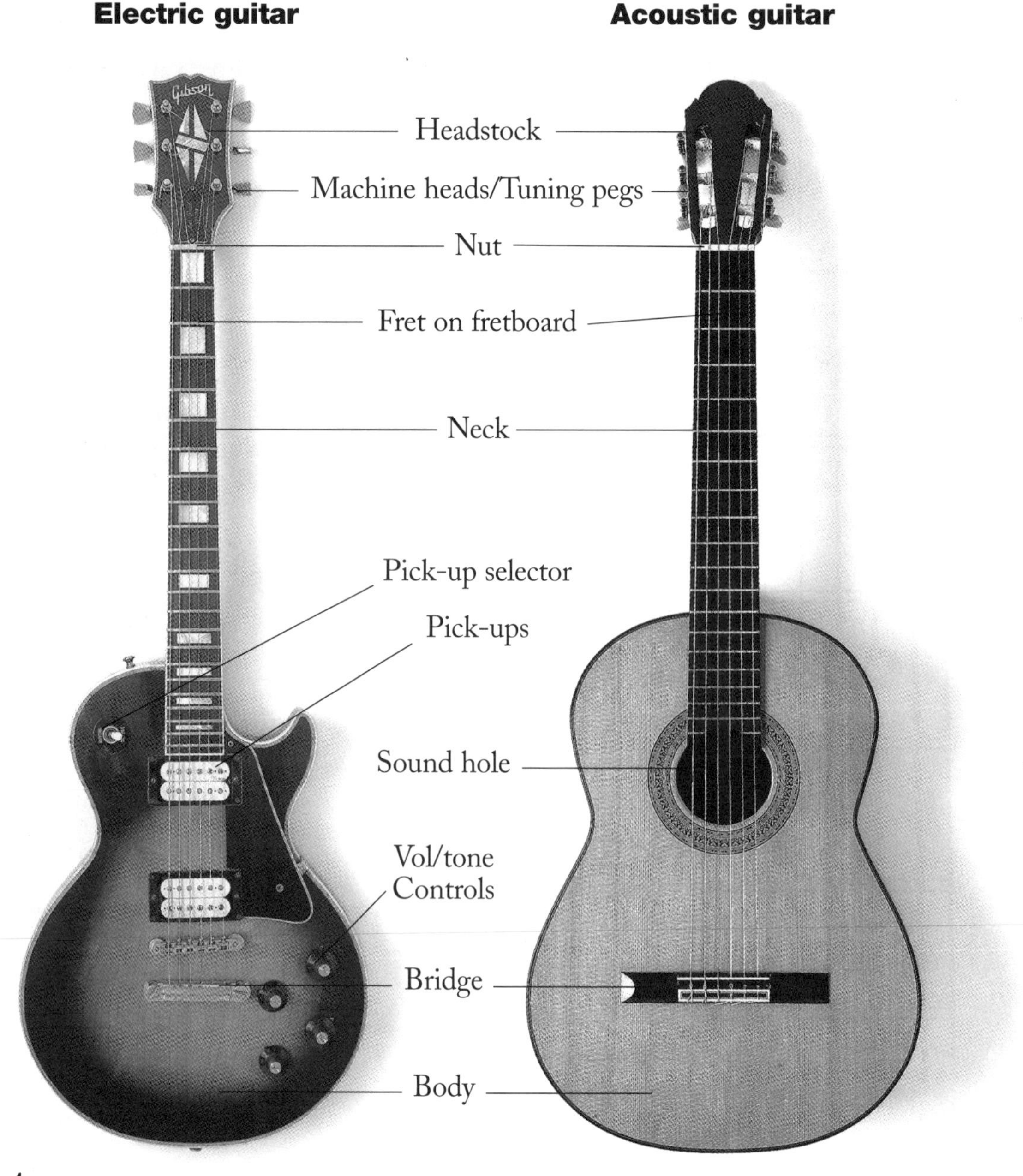

Tuning up

The most common way to tune your guitar is to use relative tuning.
This involves using the instrument's heaviest string to tune the other strings:

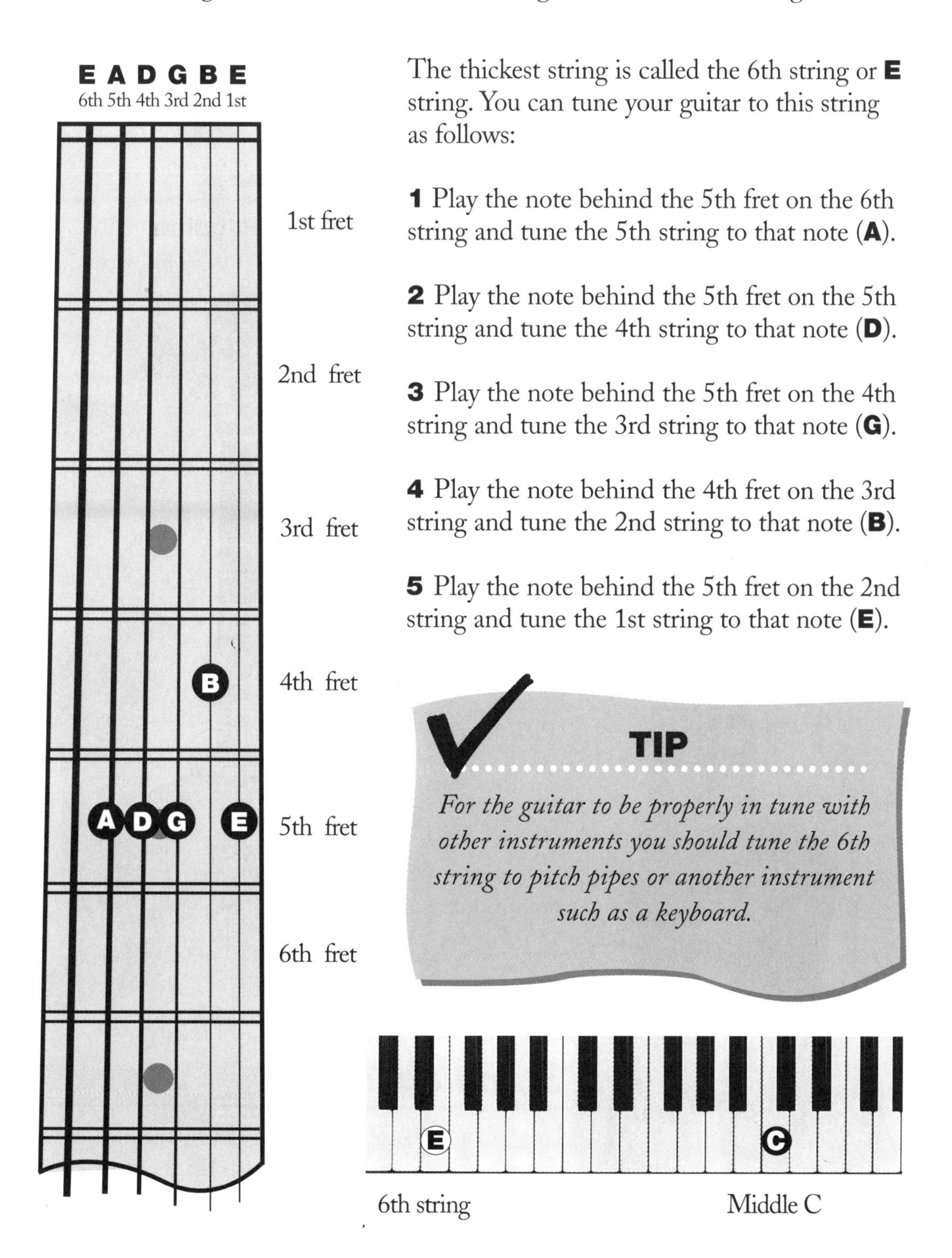

The thickest string is called the 6th string or **E** string. You can tune your guitar to this string as follows:

1 Play the note behind the 5th fret on the 6th string and tune the 5th string to that note (**A**).

2 Play the note behind the 5th fret on the 5th string and tune the 4th string to that note (**D**).

3 Play the note behind the 5th fret on the 4th string and tune the 3rd string to that note (**G**).

4 Play the note behind the 4th fret on the 3rd string and tune the 2nd string to that note (**B**).

5 Play the note behind the 5th fret on the 2nd string and tune the 1st string to that note (**E**).

TIP

For the guitar to be properly in tune with other instruments you should tune the 6th string to pitch pipes or another instrument such as a keyboard.

Holding the guitar

The first thing to remember about your posture when holding the guitar is that you should be comfortable while playing it. Sit or stand in such a way that your arms are free to play the instrument. They must not take the weight of the guitar.

Sitting down

This is the best posture for practising on the guitar; the weight of the instrument is supported in your lap, allowing your arms to move more freely.

Standing up

Use a strap to support the weight of the instrument if you're standing. You must also tilt the neck upwards to optimise your playing comfort.

Singing with the guitar

Your posture is particularly important if you want to sing while playing the guitar because you'll need to make sure that you can do both things effectively.

Make yourself as comfortable as possible so that you can perform at your very best.

You may also want to practice strumming with and without your voice. If you work on your guitar playing without singing, you can improve your playing technique.

Once you have learnt new 'chops', you can then try to incorporate them into your playing while you're singing.

Using a capo

▲ ***Fran Healy from Travis***

Sometimes you will need to use a capo in order to play along with the songs in the Chord Songbook series. The strange 'chiming' guitar sound on Travis' hit 'Driftwood' was achieved by putting a capo at the 7th fret.

A capo is simply a small device that clamps across the guitar neck, to raise the pitch of all the strings together – making it useful when transposing songs or simplifying chords. They come in different forms, from cheap, basic ones, to more sturdy types (see photo, right).

You can get one from any guitar shop – it might be the most useful accessory you ever buy!

Using a pick

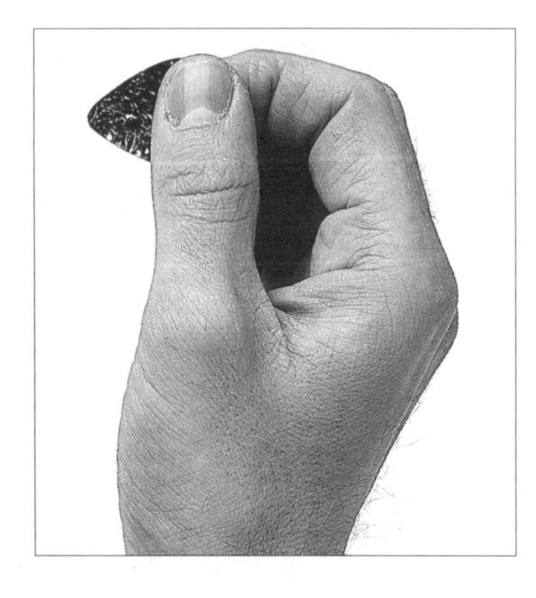

Most players hold the pick, or plectrum, between their thumb and index fingers just like in this picture.

Thick picks are particularly effective at playing single notes while thinner ones tend to be more flexible when you're strumming. Buy a variety of picks and experiment with them to see which one suits your style of playing the most.

Hold the pick firmly but not too tightly as your hand must be supple to strum rhythms effectively.

▲ ***some different picks***

Make sure there's enough of the pick showing to make good contact with the strings but also enough gripped between your thumb and forefinger to make it feel stable while strumming.

Playing a chord

Let's look at how to play a chord. For this example, we're going to play an **A** chord.

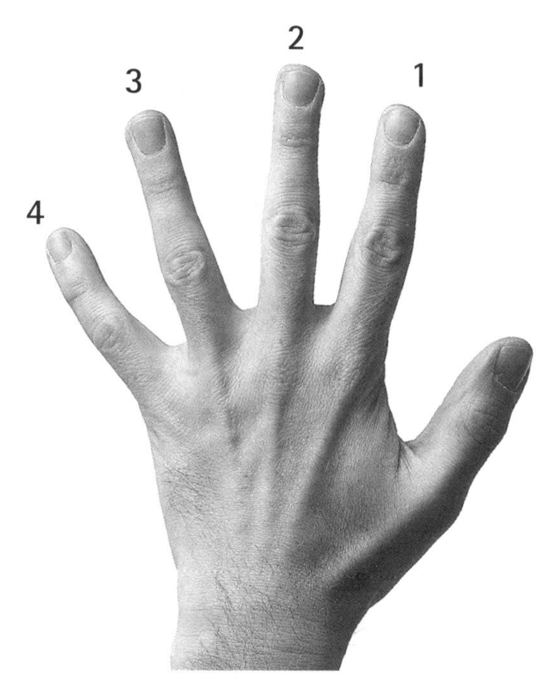

For the purposes of chord diagrams, the fingers of your fretting hand are numbered 1, 2, 3 and 4, from index to little finger.

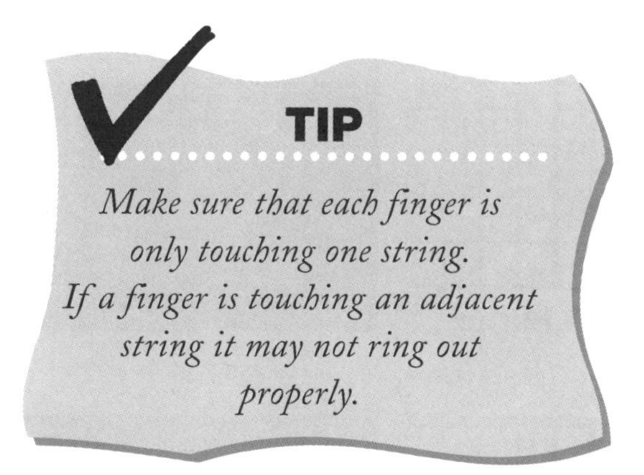

Make sure the thumb of your fretting hand is firmly gripping the back of the neck, but don't grip the neck too hard or your movement will be restricted.

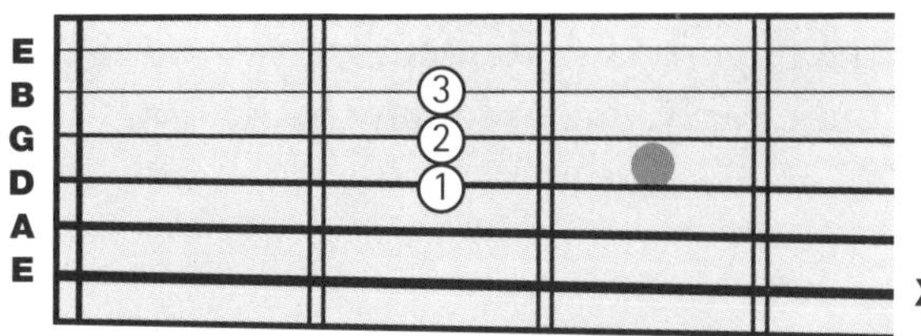

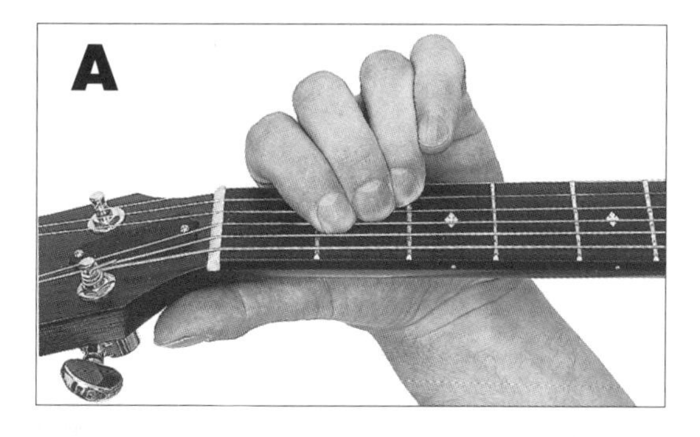

Place your first finger in the space behind the second fret on the fourth string. Then put your second finger in the same space on the third string and your third finger again in the same space on the second string. Now strum the chord, making sure that all of the notes ring out except for the thickest (sixth) string. The **x** mark next to this string in the diagram above means that you should not play the string.

▼ ***keep your thumb at the back of the neck***

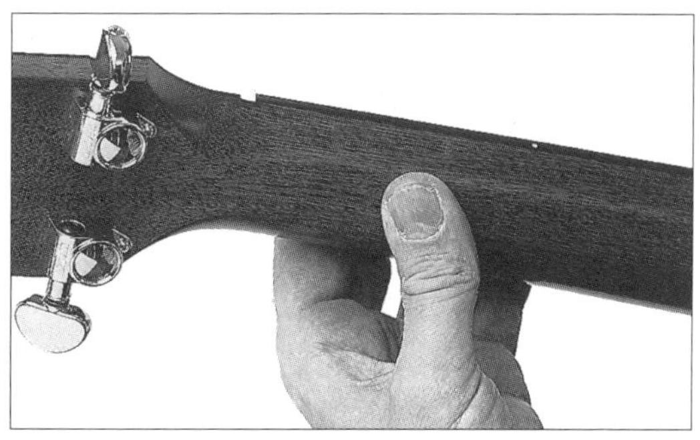

Other chords

Now that you have mastered one chord, here are some more for you to play with. Form them by putting the appropriately numbered fingers on the positions shown on the fingerboard. Remember, you want each string to ring out cleanly, except for any marked **x**.

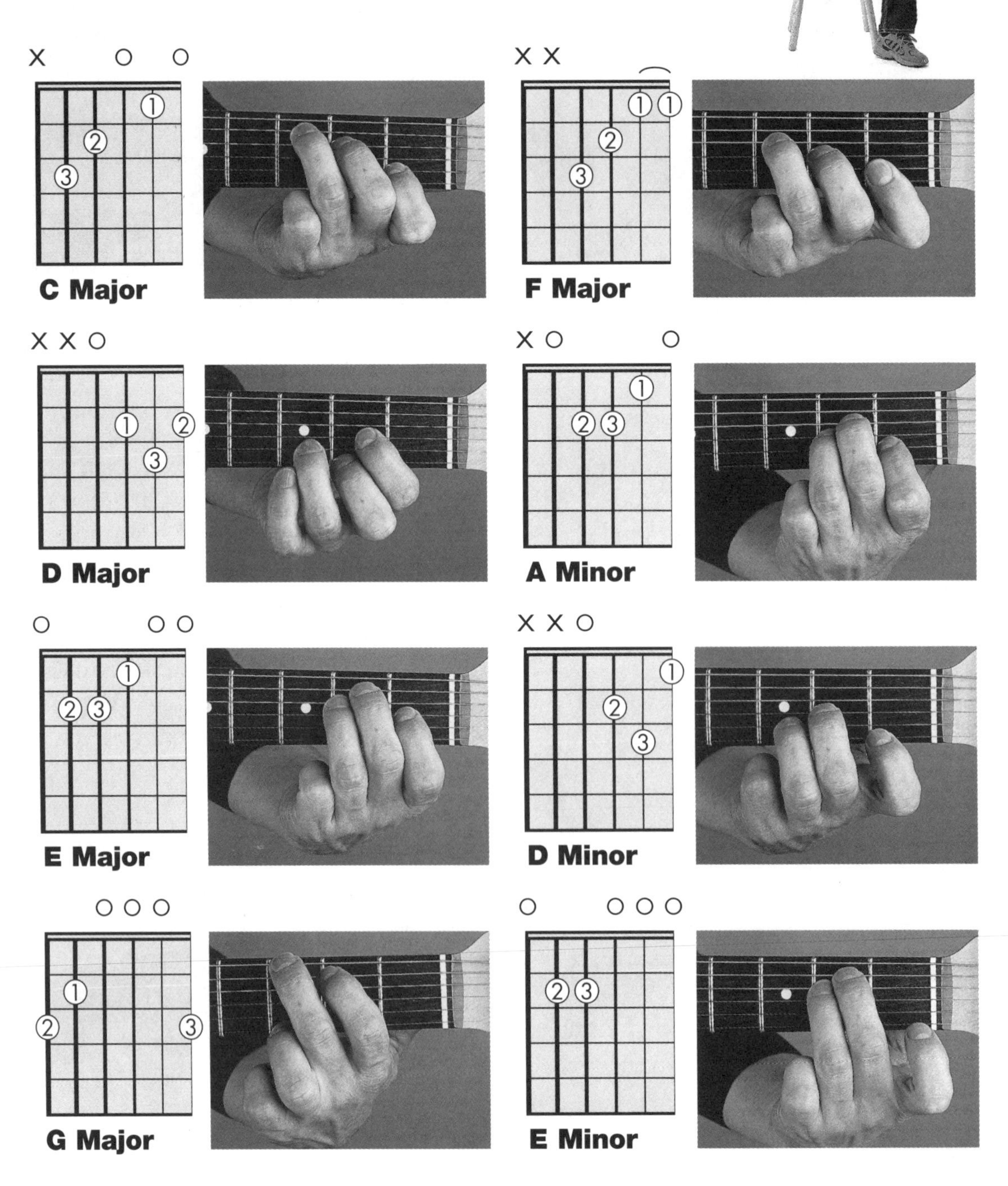

KEY

Major chords

These chords have a bright, happy sound. They are abbreviated by their alphabetical symbols (eg. **A**, **C**, **D**, **E**, **G** and **F**).

Minor chords

These chords produce a sadder sound when you strum them. They are abbreviated with a little '**m**' suffix (eg. **Am**, **Dm**, **Em**).

Seventh chords

These chords have a more bluesy feel to them. They are represented by a '**7**' suffix (eg. **A7**, **C7**, **D7**).

Barre chords

Some chords - **F** for example - can be played as barre chords. For these chords the first finger is barred right across the guitar's fingerboard. This needs to be held down firmly so that all of the notes it holds down can ring out clearly.

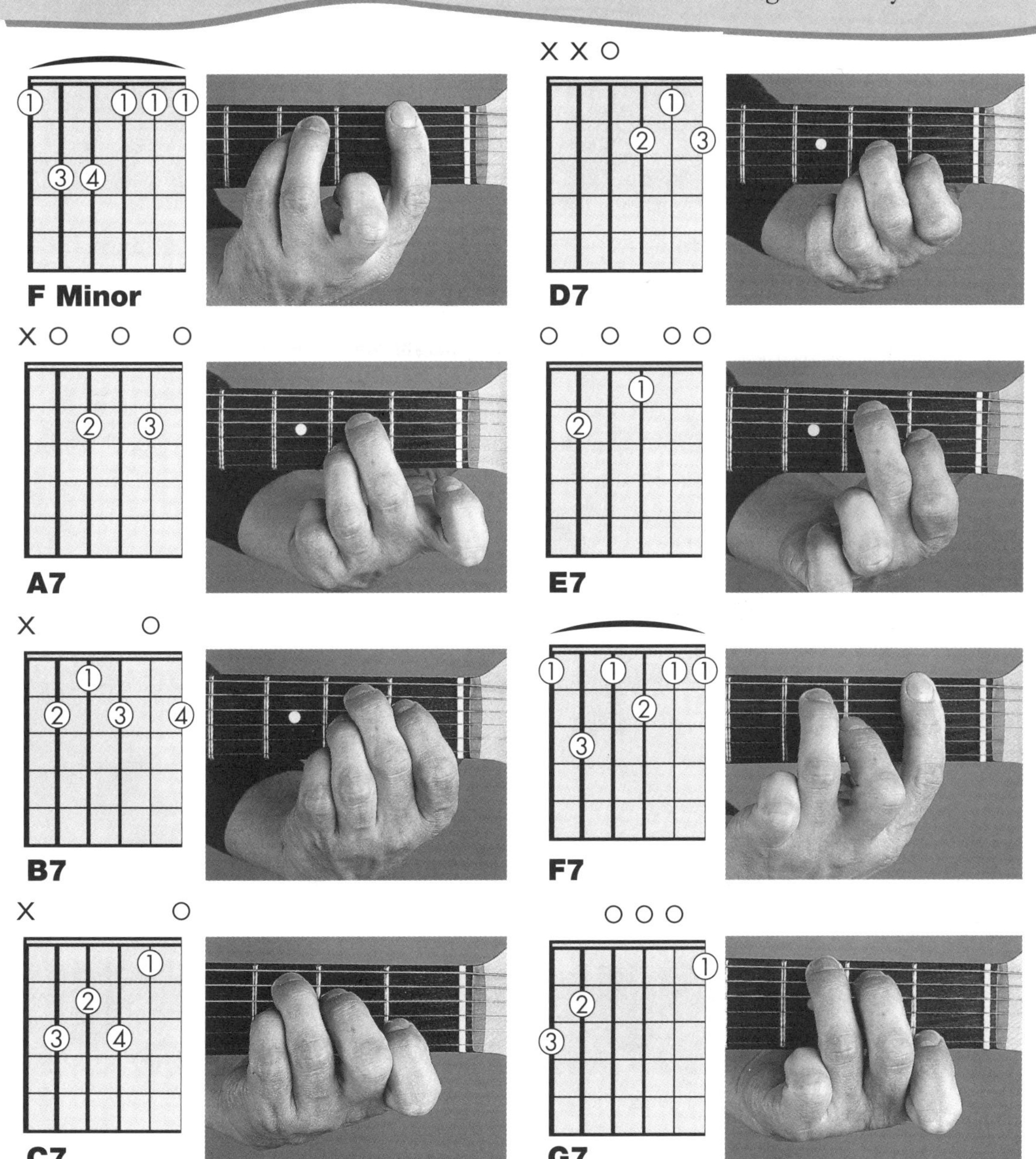

Strumming

Once you can play a chord cleanly, you can begin strumming a rhythm with it. Here are the basics…

1 Rest your forearm on the top of the guitar so it can move freely. Tilt your pick up and strum downwards, from the thickest string.

2 This above picture is like a freeze frame half way through a strum. The pick is brushing lightly down the guitar strings.

Perform the above downward strumming exercise in 4/4 (four beats to the bar) using an **A** chord. Keep your strums even and in time:

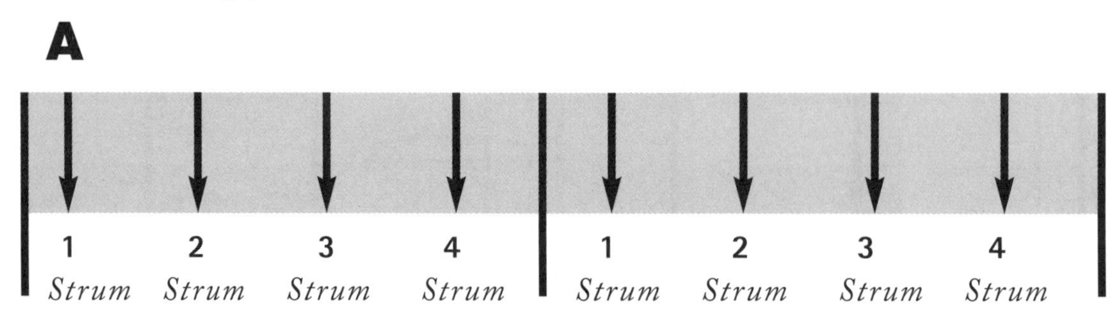

As soon as you feel comfortable with the above example, try adding upstrokes (strumming upwards) after the second and fourth beats:

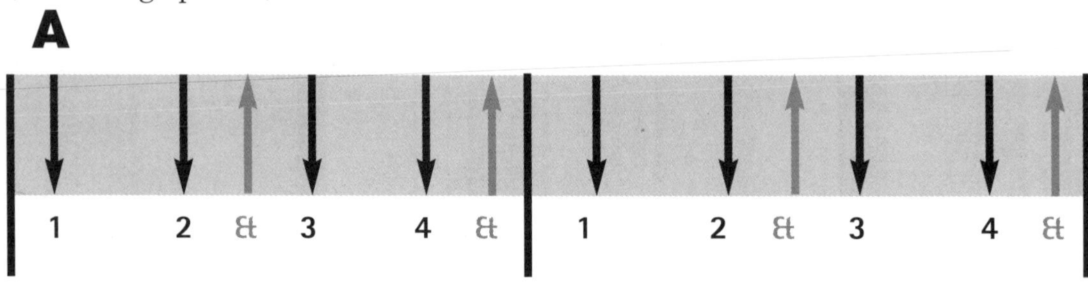

TIP

Strum along with a metronome to keep in time. Start with a slow tempo first.

3 At the end of the downward strum, the hand should stop and then immediately move back up to its original position.

4 You're now ready to begin another downward strum. Repeat your downward strumming until a smooth rhythm is obtained.

Now do the same thing using a 3/4 rhythm (three beats to every bar). Again, keep your strums even and in time:

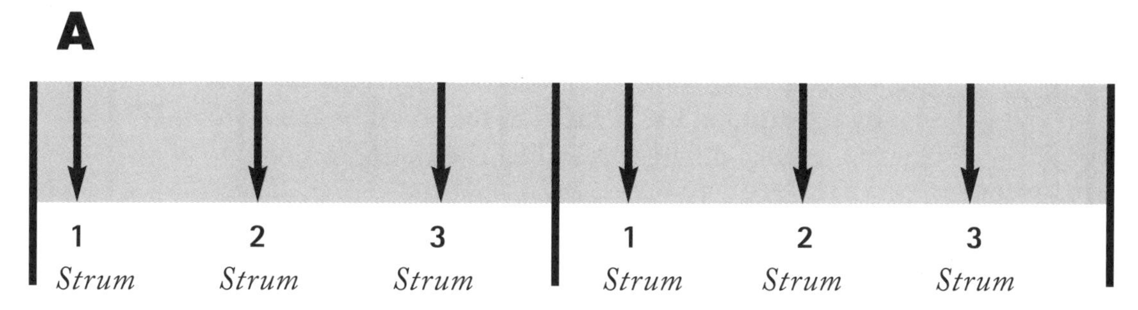

Now do the same thing using a 3/4 rhythm (three beats to every bar). Again, keep your strums even and in time:

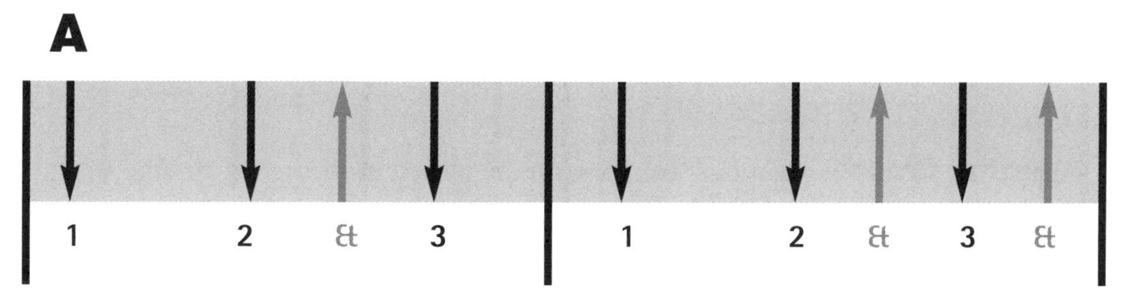

Key of A

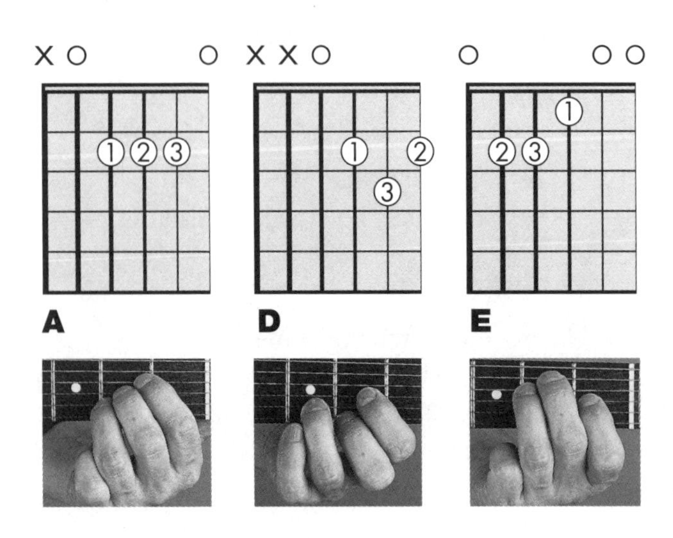

The key of **A** is one of the easiest keys to play songs in.
The three main chords in this key are **A**, **D** and **E**.

You can create a simple chord progression by strumming these three chords one after another:

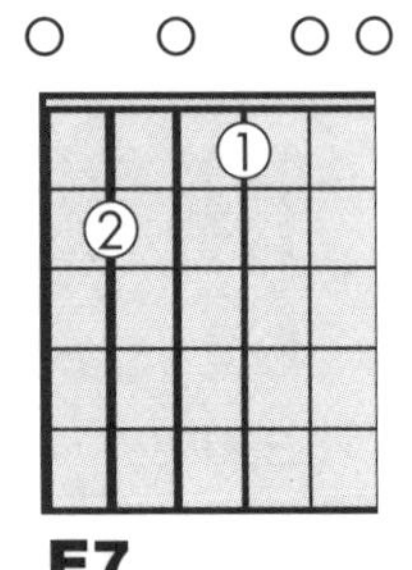

E7 is another chord that sounds good in the key of **A**.
By substituting the **E** chord in the above progression for **E7** you can create a different sounding chord progression:

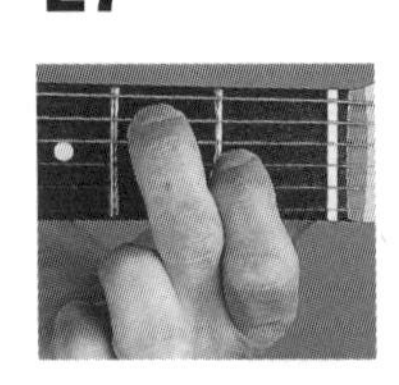

A	**D**	**E7**	**A**
Strum	*Strum*	*Strum*	*Strum*

Amazing Grace is a famous song that can be played in the key of **A**. You can create guitar accompaniment for the song simply by strumming the appropriate chords in **A** in time with specific words in the song:

Amazing Grace

Traditional

```
   A       A         D        A
A - mazing grace, how sweet the sound,

 A   A       E          E7
That saved a wretch like me.

A        A       D        A
I once was lost, but now I'm found

  A          E    A
Was blind, but now I see.
```

Once you feel comfortable with the chords, you can strum a rhythm pattern for the song. **Amazing Grace** is in 3/4 (there are three beats to every bar) and so you can play each chord with three downstrokes with your strumming hand:

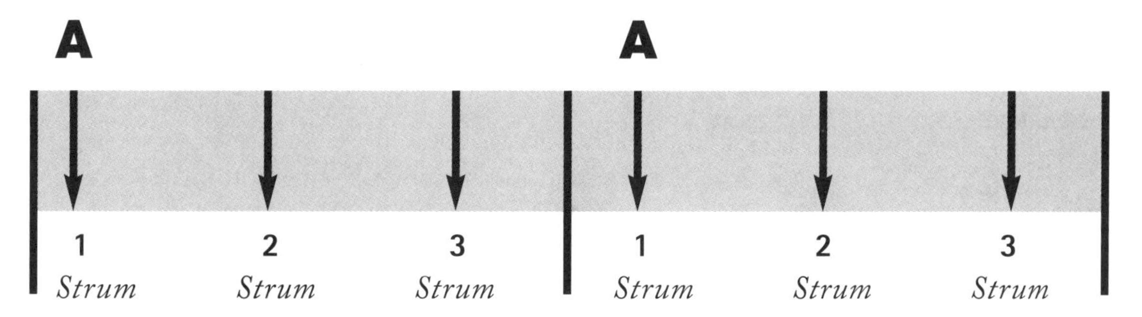

Apply this rhythm to the **Amazing Grace** chord progression and the song will come to life!

DID YOU KNOW?

Amazing Grace was a No. 1 hit in 1972 for The Pipes and Drums and Military Band of The Royal Scots Dragoon Guards. Bet that was a mouthful for the presenter of Top of The Pops!

Key of D

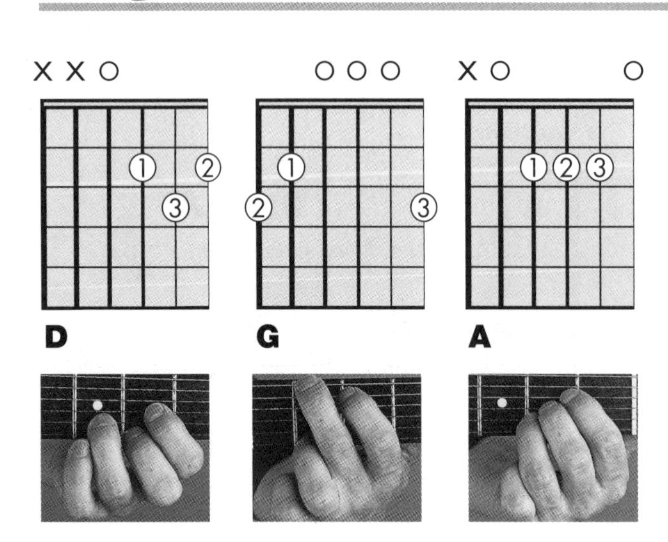

D is another easy key to play in. The three main chords in the key of **D** are **D**, **G** and **A**.
Auld Lang Syne can be played by strumming the above chords along with words underneath the chord symbols in the song:

Auld Lang Syne

Traditional

D **A**
Should auld acquaintance be forgot,

D **G**
And never brought to mind?

D **A**
Should auld acquaintance be forgot,

G **D**
For the sake of auld lang syne?

REFRAIN:

D **A**
For auld lang syne, my dear

D **G**
For auld lang syne.

D **A**
We'll take a cup of kindness yet,

G **D**
For auld lang syne.

PUB QUIZ FACT

When this song was released by Weekend in 1985, it only reached No. 47 in the pop charts. It's still known the world over as the song no-one knows the rest of the words to!

You can, if you wish, play **G7** and **A7** chords instead of **G** and **A** to give your song a 'bluesy' feel:

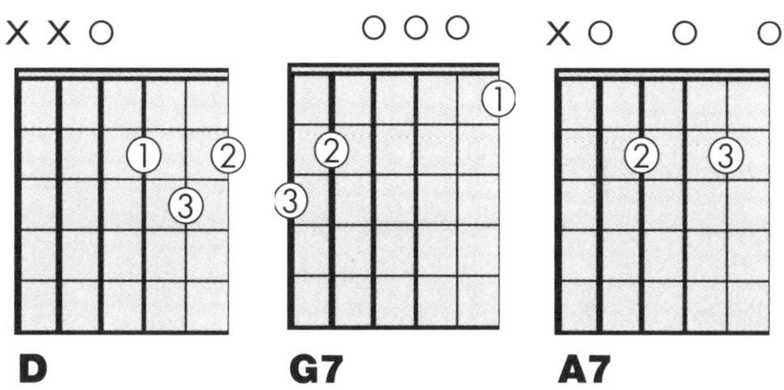

Try strumming a progression using **D**, **G7** and **A7** in 4/4 (four beats to each bar). Play a downstroke on each beat and keep on repeating it until you have nice even strumming:

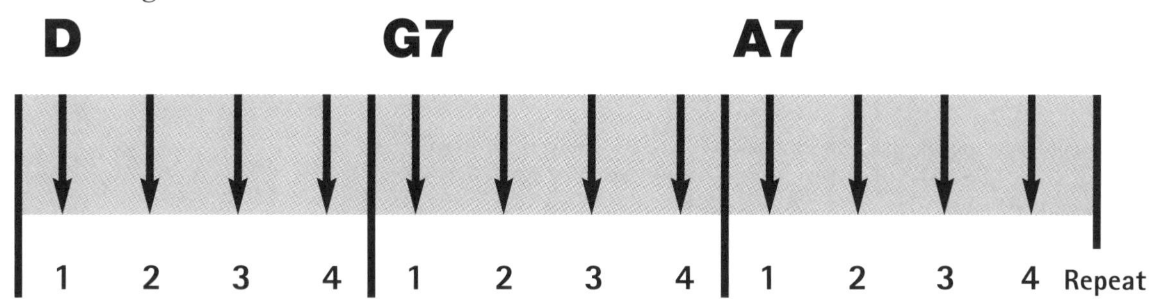

To make things a bit more lively, strum the rhythm with upstrokes after the 2nd, 3rd and 4th beats:

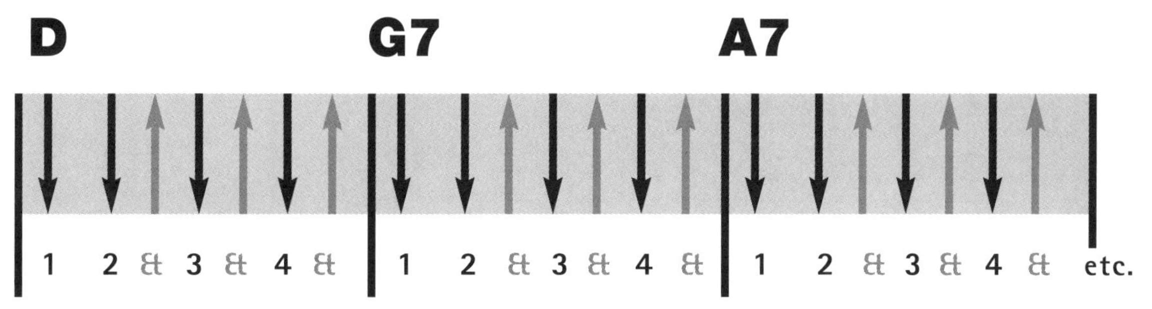

You can use these chords and this rhythm to play the verses in **Stuck In The Middle With You**, by Stealer's Wheel (see over). Simply keep the rhythm going and change chords when you get to the lyric word underneath the chord symbol in the song.

DID YOU KNOW?

Stuck In The Middle With You has been a top ten hit for both Stealer's Wheel in 1973, and Louise in 2001, but you might also recognise it from the cult movie Reservoir Dogs.

Stuck In The Middle With You

Words and music by Joe Egan & Gerry Rafferty

IST VERSE

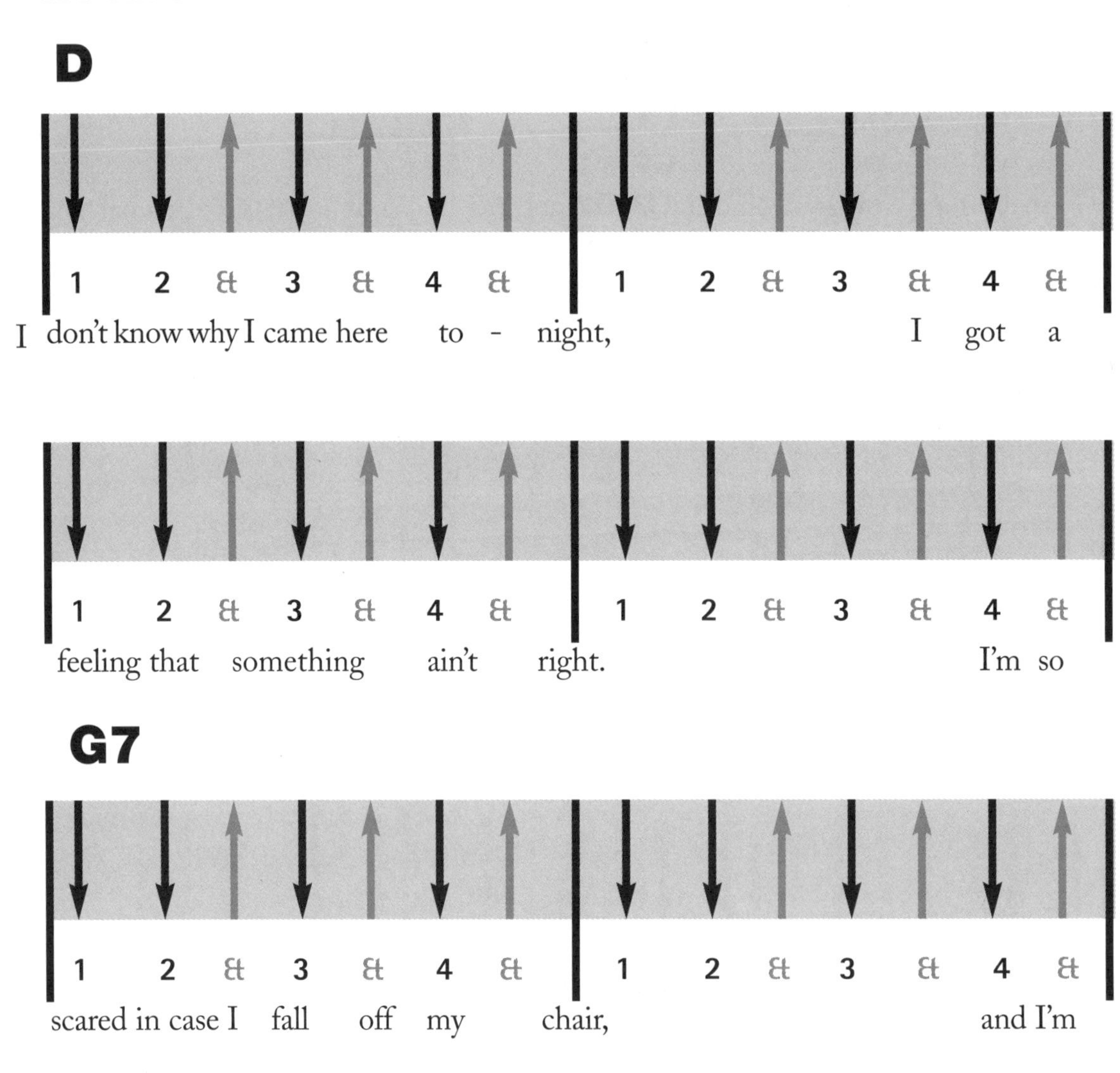

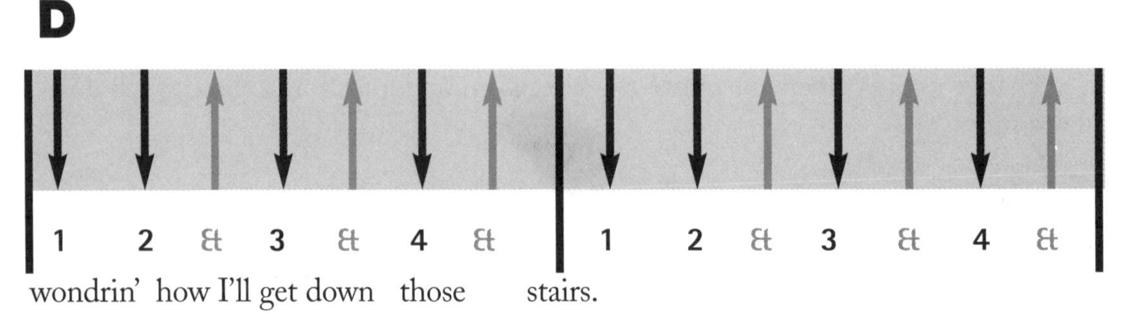

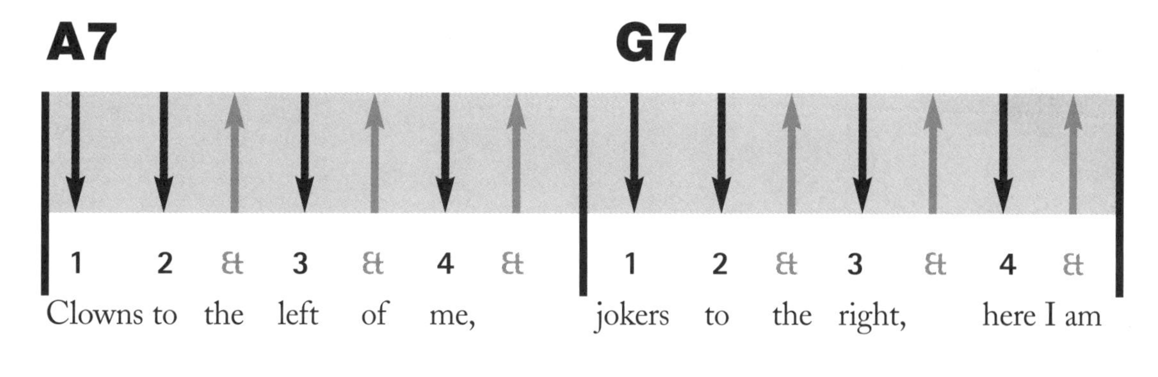

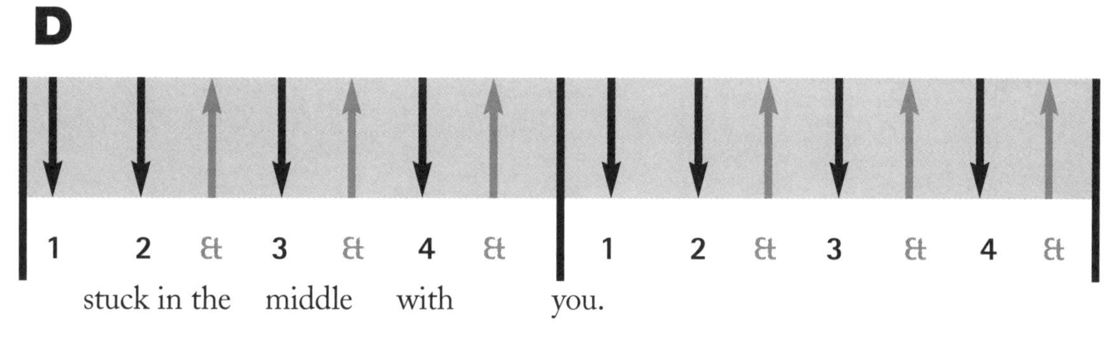

2ND VERSE
Use same rhythm as above

D
Yes I'm stuck in the middle with you,

And I'm wondering what it is I should do.

G7
It's so hard to keep the smile from my face,

D
Losing control, yeah I'm all over the place.

A7 **G7**
Clowns to the left of me, jokers to the right.

D
Here I am, stuck in the middle with you.

Bob Dylan is one of the most influential singer-songwriters of all time

Key of G

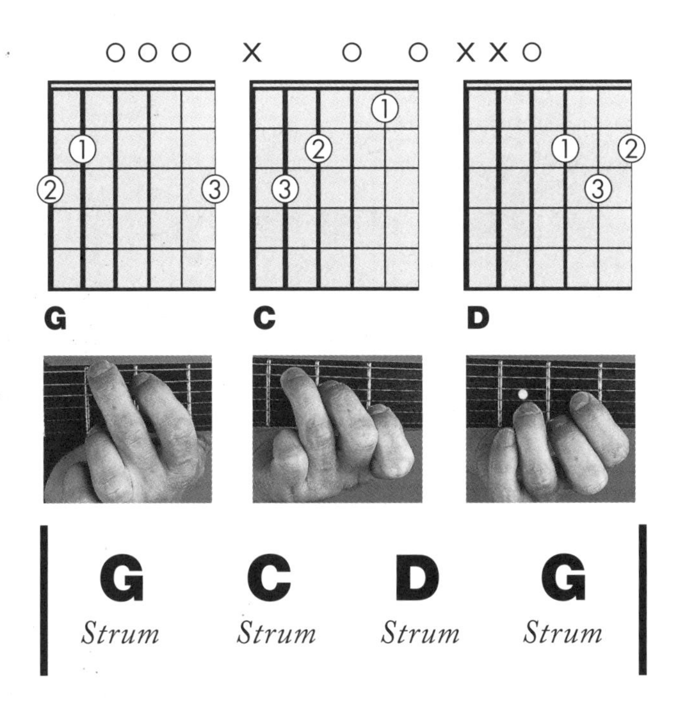

Now we come to the key of **G**. The three main chords in this key are **G**, **C** and **D**.

Strum these chords in a 4/4 rhythm with upstrokes between the 2nd and 3rd beats, and the 3rd and 4th beats:

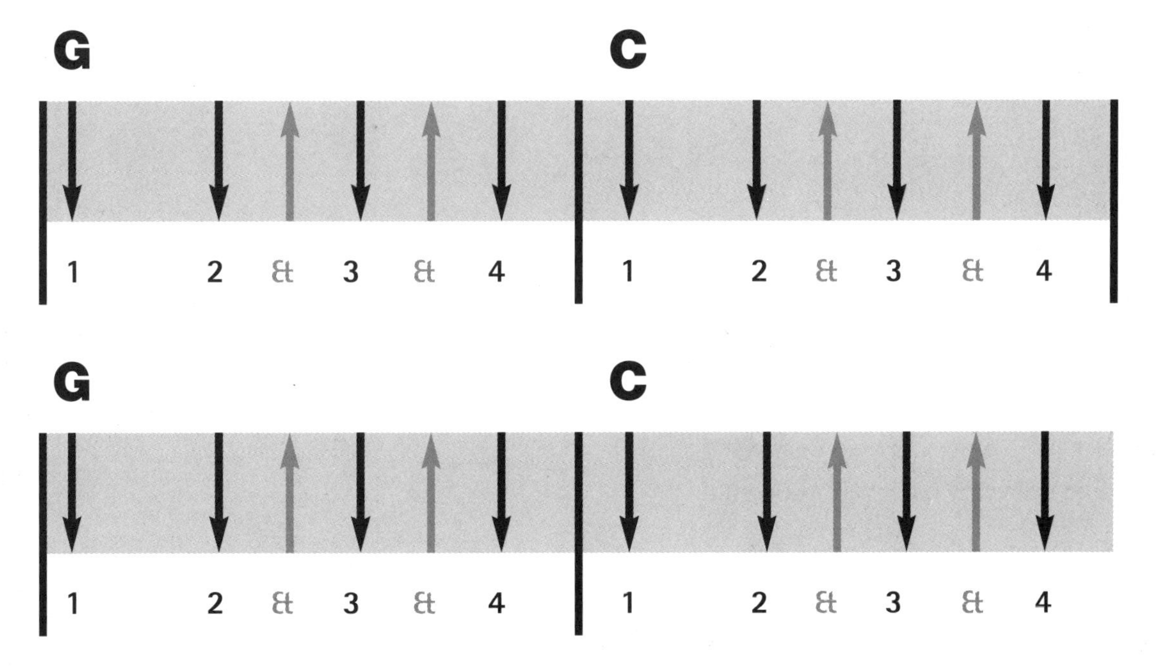

That sounds more musical, doesn't it? Now it's time to use this strumming pattern in another song. **Blowin' In The Wind**, by Bob Dylan, uses **G**, **C** and **D** chords and can be played with the rhythm you've just learnt.

Blowin' In The Wind

Words and music by Bob Dylan

IST VERSE

G C D G
How many roads must a man walk down

C G
Before you can call him a man?

C D G
How many seas must a white dove sail

C D
Before she sleeps in the sand?

G C D G
Yes, 'n' how many times must the cannon balls fly

C G
Before they're forever banned?

DID YOU KNOW?

Unusually for such a well-known song, this folk standard didn't even make it into the charts when Bob Dylan released it, but made No.13 for Peter Paul and Mary in 1963.

CHORUS

C D G C
The answer, my friend, is blowin' in the wind,

D G
The answer is blowin' in the wind.

2ND VERSE

G C D G
Yes, 'n' how many years can a mountain exist?

C G
Before it is washed to the sea?

C D G
Yes, 'n' how many years can some people exist

C D
Before they're allowed to be free?

G C D G
Yes, 'n' how many times can a man turn his head

C G
And pretend that he just doesn't see?

CHORUS:

C D G C
The answer, my friend, is blowin' in the wind,

D G
The answer is blowin' in the wind.

Clementine

Traditional

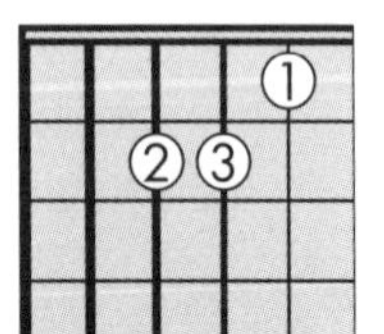

Am

Throw an **A** minor chord into a chord progression in **G** and you'll get a haunting, lyrical effect. The folk song, **Clementine**, is a good example of this:

VERSE

G
In a cavern, by a canyon,

D
Excavating for a mine,

Am G
Dwelt a miner, forty-niner,

D G
And his daughter, Clementine.

CHORUS

G
Oh, my darling, oh my darling,

D
Oh, my darling, Clementine,

Am G
You are lost and gone forever,

D G
Dreadful sorrow, Clementine.

Clementine is in 3/4 (three beats to every bar) and can be strummed in the following way:

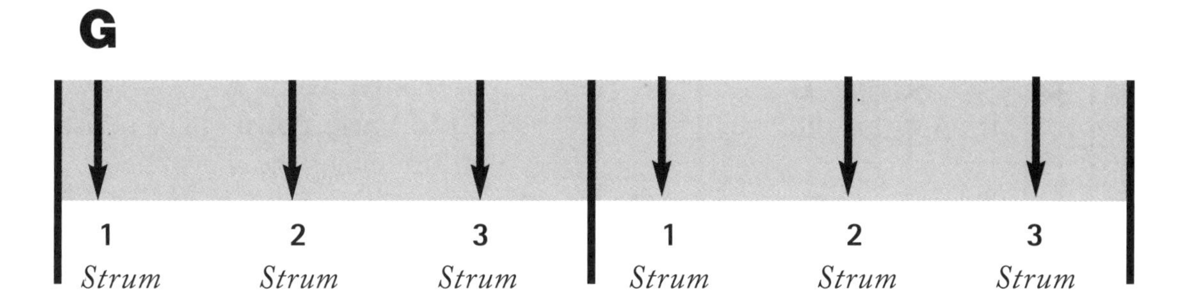

Three more chords that sound good in **G** are **E minor**, **A7** and **D7**:

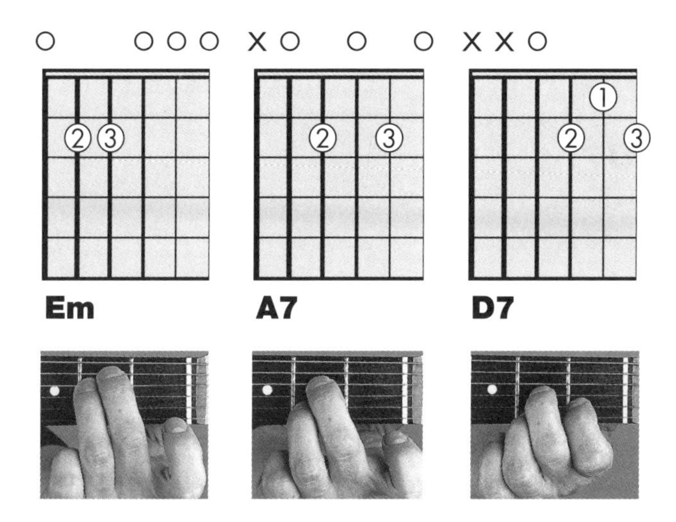

American Pie, written and originally sung by Don McLean but also a later hit for Madonna, uses these chords. A rhythm that works well with the chorus of this tune is the 4/4 one below:

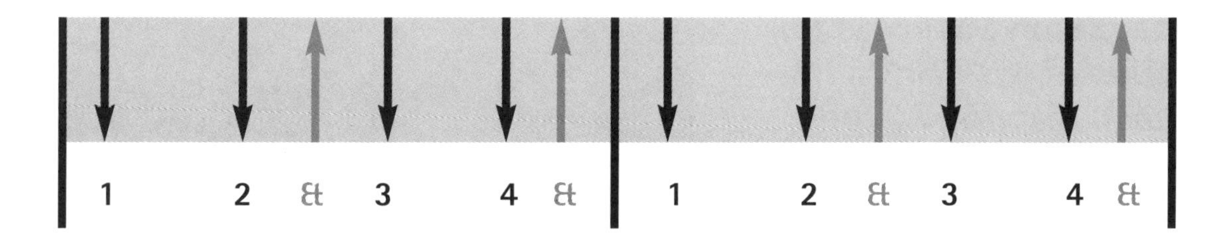

American Pie

Words and music by Don McLean

CHORUS

G C G D
Bye-bye, Miss American Pie,

G C G D
Drove my Chevy to the levee but the levee was dry.

G C G D
And them good old boys were drinkin' whiskey and rye,

Em A7
Singin' this'll be the day that I die.

Em D7
This'll be the day that I die.

TIP

You can find Don McLean's full length version in 'The Big Acoustic Guitar Chord Songbook Gold'. AM967813

Don McLean was born in New Rochelle, New York on October 2, 1945. He began his career in music as a folk singer and had a huge hit with* American Pie *in 1971. The song is said to have been inspired by the death of Buddy Holly.

▶ ***Don McLean***

Madonna's updated version of the song was a big hit, reaching No. 1 in 2000.

Key of E

The next song uses one new chord, **B7** and is in the key of **E**.

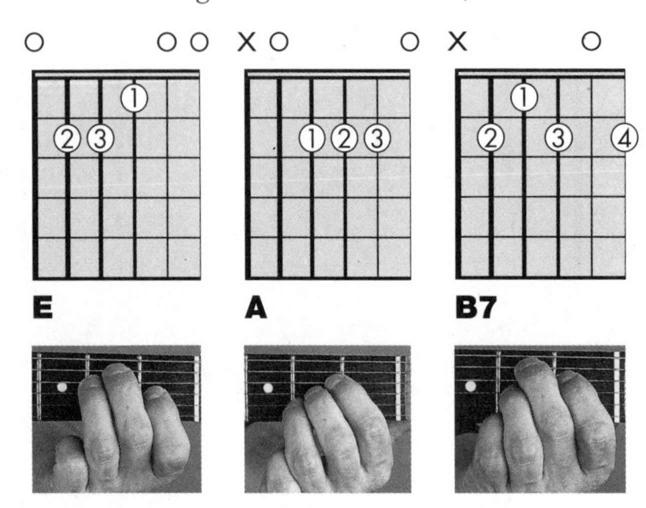

The three main guitar chords in the key of **E** are **E**, **A** and **B7**.

You might find **B7** a little tricky to play at first but, with a little bit of patience, it is really quite easy. Just practice the following chord progression and you'll master it in next to no time!

E	**A**	**B7**	**E**
Strum	*Strum*	*Strum*	*Strum*

Swing Low, Sweet Chariot

Traditional

E **A** **E**
Swing low, sweet chariot,

B7
Coming for to carry me home.

E **A** **E**
Swing low, sweet chariot,

B7 **E**
Coming for to carry me home.

DID YOU KNOW?

This song has been released by a number of different artists including Eric Clapton, and became the official England Rugby song in 1999.

Swing Low can be played in 4/4 with a basic, slow downbeat rhythm:

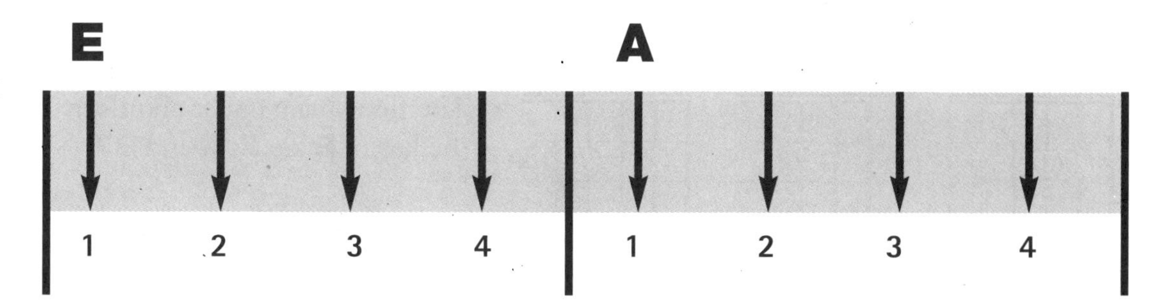

But you might prefer to add an upstroke between the 2nd and 3rd beats:

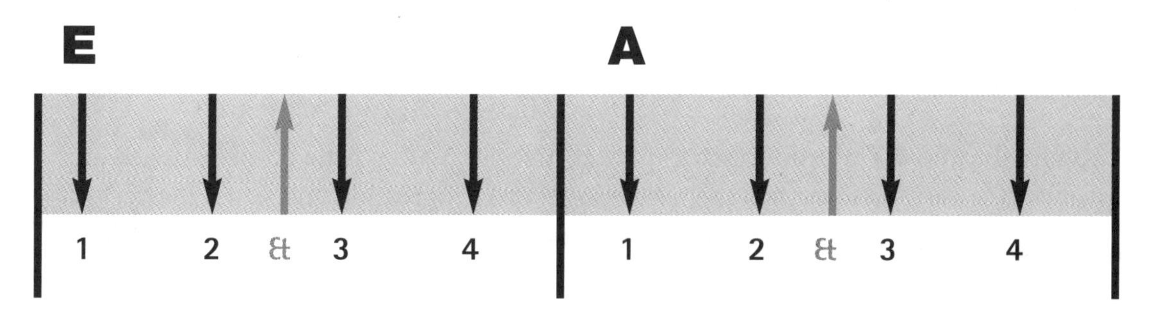

The Beatles' **Ob-La-Di, Ob-La-Da** song, on the other hand, sounds good with a busier rhythm and upstrokes after the 2nd and 4th beats:

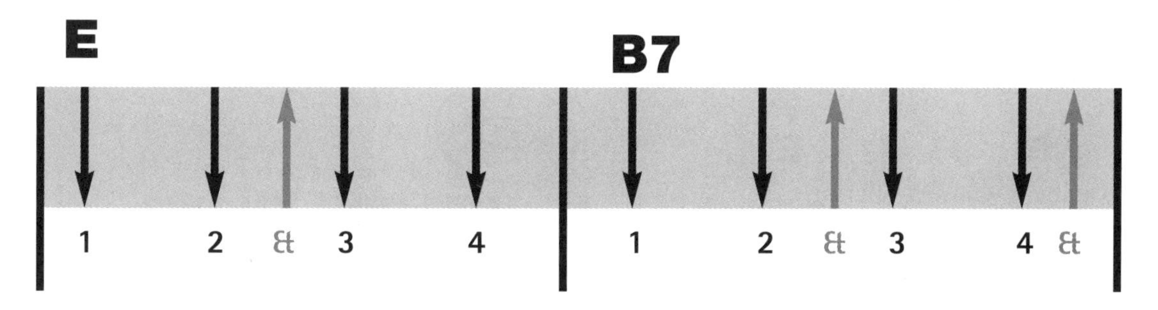

Turn the page to use the above rhythm on the famous Beatles song:

The Beatles recorded Ob-La-Di, Ob-La-Da back in 1968

Ob-La-Di, Ob-La-Da

Words and music by John Lennon and Paul McCartney

1ST VERSE

```
E                           B7
Desmond has a barrow in the market place,

                         E
Molly is the singer in a band,

                              A
Desmond says to Molly "Girl, I like your face",

            E           B7              E
And Molly says this as she takes him by the hand.
```

CHORUS

```
                             A
Ob-la-di, ob-la-da, life goes on, bra,

E            B7   E
La, la how the life goes on.

                              A
Ob-la-di, ob-la-da, life goes on, bra,

E            B7   E
La, la how the life goes on.
```

Key of C

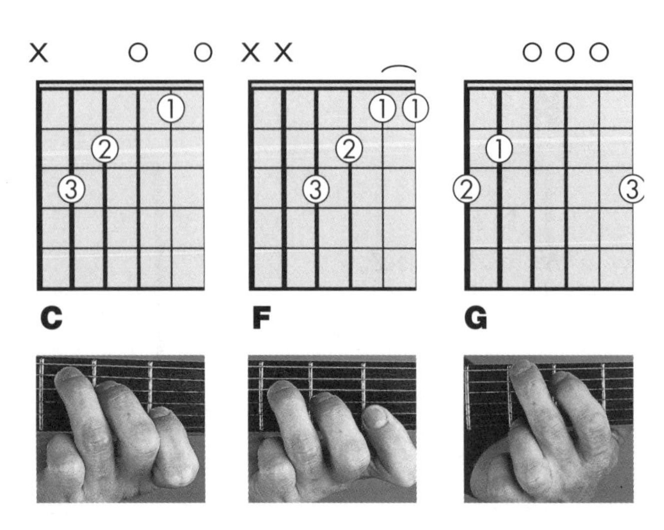

The three main chords in the key of **C** are **C**, **F** and **G**.

My Bonnie Lies Over The Ocean

Traditional

VERSE

C F C
My Bonnie lies over the ocean,

F G
My Bonnie lies over the sea,

C F C
My Bonnie lies over the ocean,

F G C
Oh, bring back my Bonnie to me.

REFRAIN

C F
Bring back, bring back,

G C
Bring back my Bonnie to me, to me.

F
Bring back, bring back,

G C
Oh, bring back my Bonnie to me.

My Bonnie works with a fairly quick 6/8 rhythm (6 short beats to each bar) with a downbeat strum on each beat:

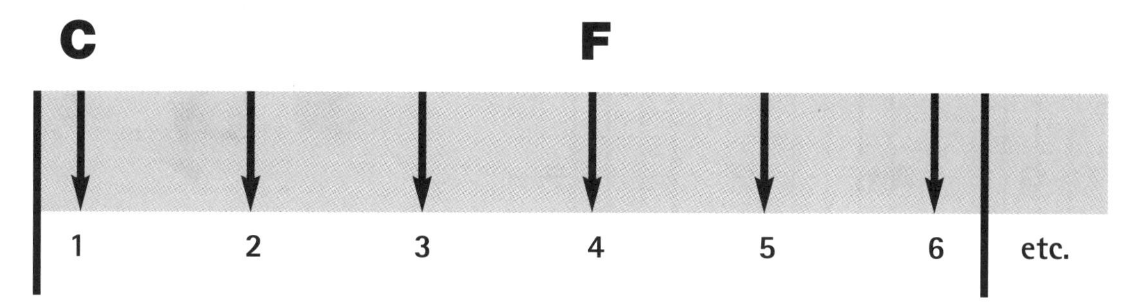

Don't Look Back In Anger

In contrast, the chorus of **Don't Look Back In Anger**, by Oasis, is complemented very well by the following 4/4 rhythm:

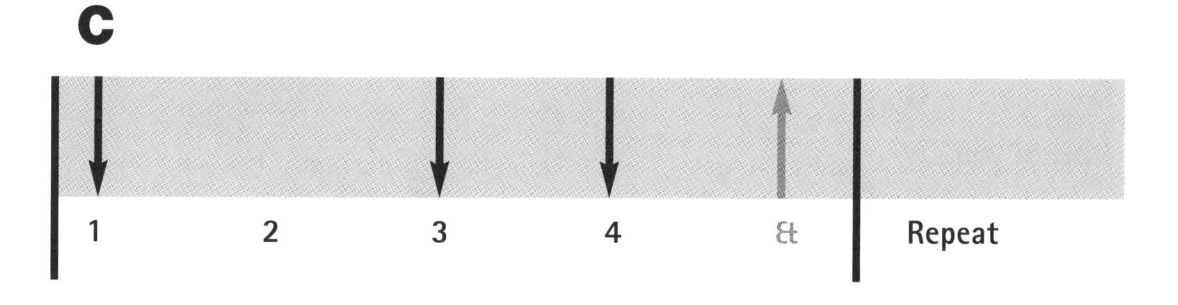

It also uses the following chords in addition to **C**, **F** and **G**:

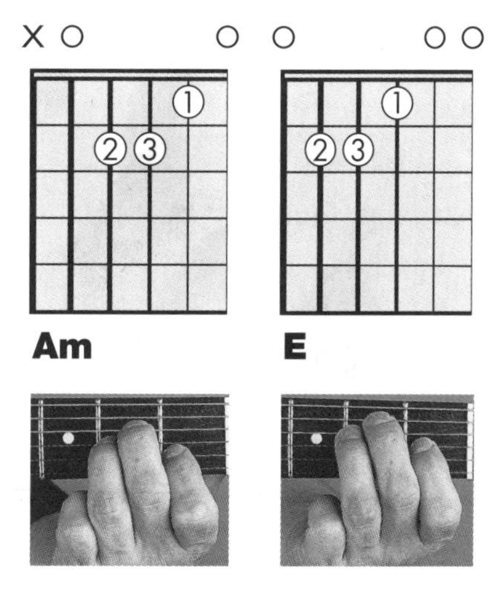

Don’t Look Back In Anger

Words and music by Noel Gallagher

CHORUS

C G Am E F
So Sally can wait, she knows it’s too late

G C Am G
As she’s walking on by.

C G Am E F
Her soul slides away, but don’t look back in anger

G C
I heard you say.

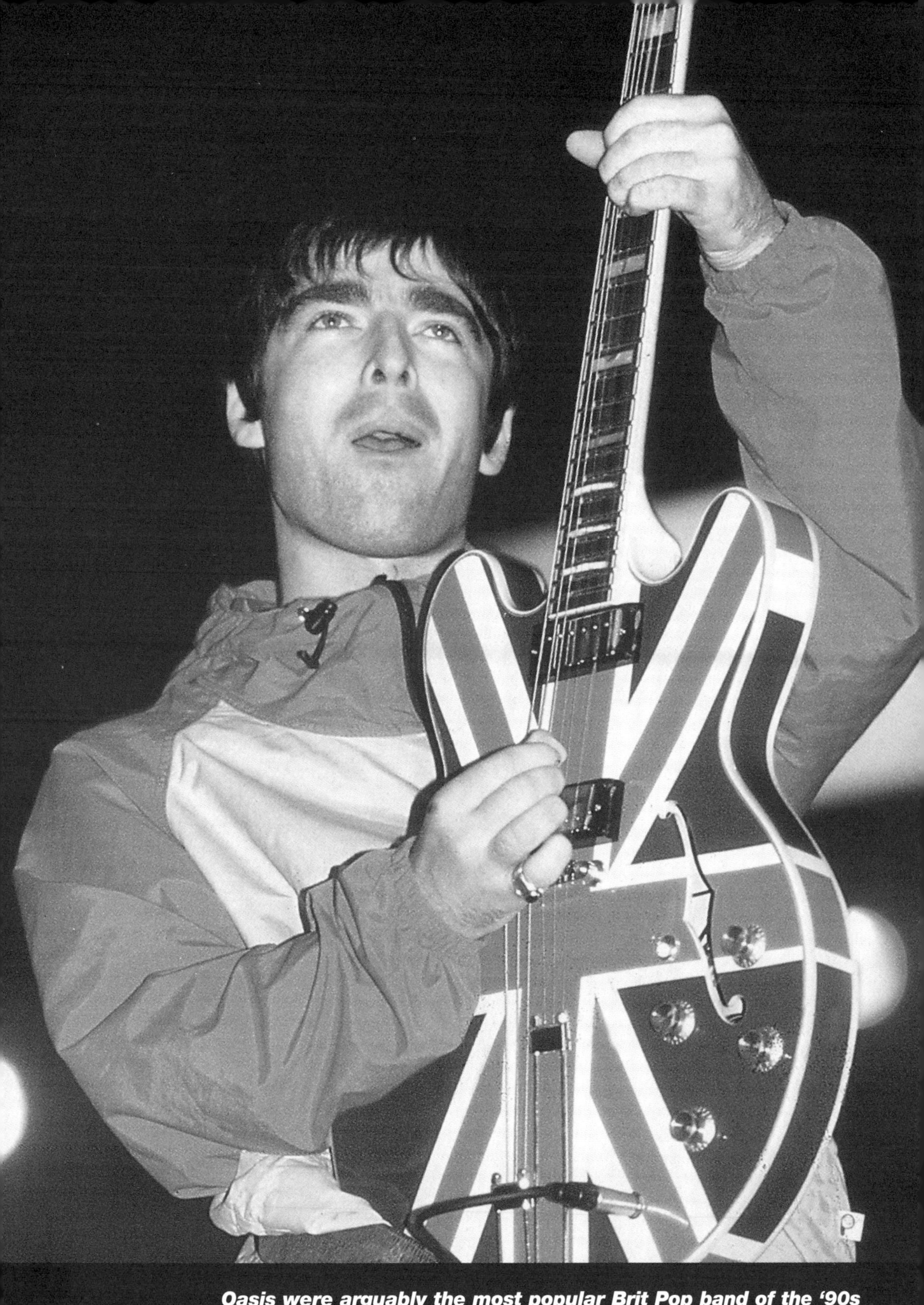

Oasis were arguably the most popular Brit Pop band of the '90s

Simon & Garfunkel recorded a popular version of the traditional folk song, Scarborough Fair, in the 1960s

Minor keys

Although many popular songs are in major keys, some are in minor ones. These songs have more minor chords in them:

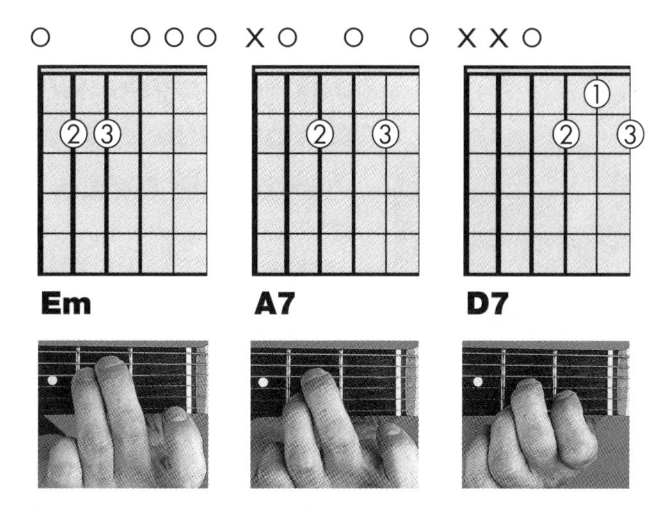

This version of the popular folk song, **Scarborough Fair**, is arranged in the key of **D minor**:

Scarborough Fair

Traditional

Dm **Am** **Dm**
Where are you going; to Scarborough Fair?

G **Dm**
Parsley, sage, rosemary and thyme.

F **C**
Remember me to a bonny lass there,

Dm **G** **Am** **Dm**
For she was once a true love of mine.

TIP

You can play the full-length version of this song from the 'Simon & Garfunkel' chord songbook. PS11524

Play all these Simon & Garfunkel hits with just a few easy chords for each song!
Simon & Garfunkel
The Chord Songbook

This song works well with a 6/8 rhythm like this:

Dm

↓	↓	↓	↓	↓	↓	
1	2	3	4	5	6	etc.

Tips on playing other songs

If you have read through all of the pages in this book so far, you will now be familiar with all of the popular keys and you will find it easier to learn new songs.

- You will also be familiar with some of the most easy strum patterns. The same principles apply to most songs, so you should now be able to work out strum patterns for most of the songs in our Chord Songbook range.

- If you're not sure, don't panic: just listen to the rhythm of a song; is it in 4/4 or 3/4? If you can count four beats for each line in a song then it is probably in 4/4, while if you find yourself counting in threes when you listen to a tune, you can bet that it's in 3/4 or 6/8. Apply the patterns in this book to the new songs and experiment with new ones.

If you come across a tricky chord, spend some extra time just practising that chord. You will find that all chords in songbooks are playable - some just require a little more practise than others.

- Play along with the original recordings as often as you can. That way you can get a much better feel for the correct rhythm and tempo of the songs, and can achieve more authentic results.

Practise a little every day. This will strengthen your fingers and make you more familiar with the feel of the guitar, the chords and the rhythms.

- Oh, and have fun too!

Chord Songbooks

Congratulations!

You now know enough to be able to confidently play through many of the songs in the huge range of chord songbooks, available from Music Sales.

There are a number of chord picture books also available, which will help you when you come across chords you're not familiar with. Below are a couple of recommended titles, and a list of just some of the music you can now play from the chord songbook series. You can order these, and many more, from all good music and book retailers, or direct from Music Sales (see page 2). Happy playing!

Title	Code
The Gig Bag Book Of Picture Chords	AM931238
The Black Book: Instant Guitar Chords	AM953414

Title	Code
60s Chord Songbook	AM967846
70s Chord Songbook	AM967857
80s Chord Songbook	AM967868
90s Chord Songbook	AM959728
Abba Chord Songbook	AM959740
AC/DC Chord Songbook	AM963501
Alanis Morissette Chord Songbook	AM944086
Ash Chord Songbook	AM957528
Beatles Chord Songbook	NO90664
Beatles Complete Chord Songbook	NO90690
Beautiful South Chord Songbook	AM959739
Bee Gees Chord Songbook	AM963556
Big Acoustic Guitar Chord Songbook	AM962192
Big Acoustic Guitar Chord Songbook **Gold**	AM967813
Big Acoustic Guitar Chord Songbook **Platinum**	AM968726
Blur Chord Songbook	AM936914
Bob Dylan Chord Songbook	AM959706
Bob Marley Chord Songbook	AM956109
Bon Jovi Chord Songbook	AM936892
Boyzone Chord Songbook	AM956956
Bryan Adams Chord Songbook	AM963490
Catatonia Chord Songbook	AM958463
Eric Clapton Chord Songbook	AM956054

Coldplay Chord Songbook AM970904
The Corrs Chord Songbook AM956967
Country Chord Songbook AM959750
Cranberries Chord Songbook AM944383
Dire Straits Chord Songbook DG70834
Elvis Presley Chord Songbook AM956043
John Lennon Chord Songbook AM956110

Kinks Chord Songbook AM956131
Kula Shaker Chord Songbook AM957539
Leonard Cohen Chord Songbook AM963480
Levellers Chord Songbook AM951445
Love Songs Chord Songbook AM959761
Meatloaf Chord Songbook AM963534
Metallica Chord Songbook AM944680

Oasis Be Here Now Chord Songbook AM950763
Oasis Chord Songbook AM936903
Oasis Chord Songbook **Two** AM951478
Oasis Complete Chord Songbook AM964502
Paul Simon Chord Songbook PS11485
Paul Weller Chord Songbook AM942546
Police Chord Songbook AM971223

Pop Chord Songbook **One** AM957891
Pop Chord Songbook **Two** AM957902
Pop Chord Songbook **Three** AM957913
Pop Chord Songbook **Four** AM957924
Pulp Chord Songbook AM942678
Shania Twain Chord Songbook AM963545
Simon & Garfunkel Chord Songbook PS11524

Smashing Pumpkins Chord Songbook AM951489
Soul Chord Songbook AM966108
Stereophonics Chord Songbook AM956065
Stone Roses Chord Songbook AM951490
Stone Roses Complete Chord Songbook AM966185
Suede Chord Songbook AM951500
Travis Chord Songbook AM963897
Wet Wet Wet Chord Songbook AM938135
The Who Chord Songbook AM956021